GALE
CENGAGE Learning

MW00582996

Nonfiction Classics for Students, Volume 2

Staff

Editor: Elizabeth Thomason.

Contributing Editors: Reginald Carlton, Anne Marie Hacht, Michael L. LaBlanc, Ira Mark Milne, Jennifer Smith.

Managing Editor, Literature Content: Dwayne D. Hayes.

Managing Editor, Literature Product: David Galens.

Publisher, Literature Product: Mark Scott.

Content Capture: Joyce Nakamura, *Managing Editor*. Sara Constantakis, *Editor*.

Research: Victoria B. Cariappa, *Research Manager*. Cheryl Warnock, *Research Specialist*. Tamara Nott, Tracie A. Richardson, *Research Associates*. Nicodemus Ford, Sarah Genik, Timothy Lehnerer, Ron Morelli, *Research Assistants*.

Permissions: Maria Franklin, *Permissions Manager*. Shalice Shah-Caldwell, *Permissions Associate*. Jacqueline Jones, *Permissions Assistant*.

Manufacturing: Mary Beth Trimper, *Manager, Composition and Electronic Prepress*. Evi Seoud, *Assistant Manager, Composition Purchasing and Electronic Prepress*. Stacy Melson, *Buyer*.

Imaging and Multimedia Content Team: Barbara Yarrow, *Manager*. Randy Bassett, *Imaging Supervisor*. Robert Duncan, Dan Newell, *Imaging Specialists*. Pamela A. Reed, *Imaging Coordinator*. Leitha Etheridge-Sims, Mary Grimes, David G. Oblender, *Image Catalogers*. Robyn V. Young, *Project Manager*. Dean Dauphinais, *Senior Image Editor*. Kelly A. Quin, *Image Editor*.

Product Design Team: Kenn Zorn, *Product Design Manager*. Pamela A. E. Galbreath, *Senior Art Director*. Michael Logusz, *Graphic Artist*.

Copyright Notice

agency, institution, publication, service, or individual does not imply endorsement of the editors or publisher. Errors brought to the attention of the publisher and verified to the satisfaction of the publisher will be corrected in future editions.

This publication is a creative work fully protected by all applicable copyright laws, as well as by misappropriation, trade secret, unfair competition, and other applicable laws. The authors and editors of this work have added value to the underlying factual material herein through one or more of the following: unique and original selection, coordination, expression, arrangement, and classification of the information. All rights to this publication will be vigorously defended.

Narrative of the Life of Frederick Douglass

Frederick Douglass 1845

Introduction

In 1838, at the age of twenty, Frederick Douglass escaped slavery and settled in the North. He quickly became involved in the campaign against slavery, known as the abolitionist movement. Seven years later in 1845, he published the *Narrative of the Life of Frederick Douglass, An American Slave, Written by Himself,* in which he told the story of his life under slavery. His moving account of slavery and his eventual escape lent a certain authenticity to Douglass' speeches and writings against institutionalized slavery that white abolitionists did not have. His use of vivid language in depicting violence against slaves, his psychological insights into the power dynamics between slaves and slaveholders, and his naming of specific persons and places made his book a powerful indictment against a society (both in the North and South of the United States) that continued to condone slavery as a viable social and economic institution.

More than a story about the evils of slavery, the *Narrative* touches on basic issues and themes important to all Americans. These include the value of freedom, social justice and equal rights, and condemnation of violence against those who do not have the legal power to protect themselves. Written in a lucid and passionate style, the *Narrative* uses a variety of rhetorical and literary devices. Teachers use it as an example of a historical document and a literary work. The *Narrative* has taken its place in the American literary canon as a precursor of a rich tradition of African-American autobiographical works, from Richard Wright's *Black Boy* to Malcolm X's (with Alex Haley) *The Autobiography of Malcolm X* and Maya Angelou's *I Know Why the Caged Bird Sings.*

Author Biography

Born on a plantation in Talbot County, Maryland, in February 1818, Frederick Douglass is best known as an orator and writer who campaigned and fought against the institution of slavery and its dehumanizing effects on African Americans. His remarkable first work, entitled *Narrative of the Life of Frederick Douglass, An American Slave, Written by Himself*, was published in 1845. It chronicles his life as a slave and his dreams of, and eventual escape to, freedom.

As a young boy, Douglass experienced and witnessed the brutal consequences of slavery. At birth, he was separated from his mother, whom he saw only a handful of times until she died when he was seven. As a young boy he was sent to Baltimore to work as a house slave. There, he was fortunate to be taught briefly how to read until his master ended his lessons. For years, Douglass continued by surreptitious means to learn how to read and write through establishing relations with Anglo society. After his master died (a man rumored to be his father), Douglass returned to rural Maryland, where he became a field hand, enduring physical and mental hardship under several different slave masters. However, he continued to educate himself and other slaves by setting up a Sunday school where he carried out lessons.

Douglass' first attempt to escape with several

of his fellow slaves was foiled. After being jailed briefly, through fortunate circumstances Douglass ended up in Baltimore, where he worked as a caulker in a shipyard. At the age of twenty, Douglass again attempted escape and this time succeeded. On his arrival in New York in 1838, he married his fiancée, Anna Murray, a free woman who worked as a domestic servant in Baltimore, and they moved to New Bedford, Massachusetts.

Douglass quickly became involved in the abolitionist movement, first in the African-American churches of New England and then among Anglo-American society after his antislavery autobiography, *Narrative of the Life of Frederick Douglass*, was published. Because of the narrative's tremendous popularity, Douglass feared that he might be in danger of re-enslavement. He traveled to England and Ireland and remained there for two years, eventually buying his freedom before returning to the United States.

On his return from the British Isles, Douglass settled in Rochester, New York, and started his own antislavery paper, the *North Star*. He also lectured around the country, continuing to publish antislavery tracts and to write his autobiography. Some of his other publications include the speech "What to the Slave Is the Fourth of July" (1852), a novella, *The Heroic Slave*, and his autobiography, *The Life and Times of Frederick Douglass* (1892). During the Civil War, Douglass tried to convince the Union government that the abolishment of slavery should be its main goal. He also encouraged and helped the U.S. government recruit African Americans to fight for the Union.

After the Civil War, Douglass continued to campaign for African-American rights as well as women's rights. His move to Washington, D.C., in 1872 placed him in close proximity to the seat of the U.S. government. He took a number of different governmental positions (under a number of different presidents), including marshal for the District of Columbia and consul general to Haiti in 1889. After his wife, Anna, died in 1882, he married Helen Pitts, a white woman who worked for him. They spent a few years traveling in Europe and northern Africa in the 1880s. In 1895, Frederick Douglass died of heart failure in Washington, D.C., on February 20. He was buried in Mount Hope Cemetery, Rochester, New York.

Preface

Before the *Narrative of the Life of Frederick Douglass: An American Slave* begins, the reader is provided with a preface, written in 1884 by the famous abolitionist leader William Lloyd Garrison, that sets the tone of the book. Garrison notes how he first met Douglass at an antislavery convention in Nantucket, Massachusetts. He then goes on to describe Douglass' impassioned and unforgettable speech that eventually led to writing this book. His thoughts echo those of many who saw Douglass speak that day when he writes, "I think that I never hated slavery so intensely as at that moment." Garrison explains how he encouraged Douglass to become involved in the abolitionist movement and how Douglass feared that he would do more harm than good. However, Garrison persisted and Douglass became one of the most eloquent and persuasive promoters of slave independence. Garrison notes that "As a public speaker, he excels in pathos, wit, comparison, imitation, strength of reasoning, and fluency of language."

In his preface, Garrison mentions a number of abolitionists who were well known in the antislavery movement. These include John A. Collins; Charles Lenox Remond, an African-American free man; and Daniel O'Connell, who fought for Irish independence in the mid-nineteenth century. These men have all argued passionately and eloquently for the end of oppression, yet Garrison claims that none is as forceful a speaker as Douglass because none has ever been a slave. Douglass' statements ring true because he has lived and breathed the tales he tells.

Garrison's purpose in writing this preface seems twofold. He wants to make a special plea to readers of Douglass' narrative that what they are reading is the real and true thing. Garrison focuses on how Douglass does not shy away from recounting names, places, and dates of events that occurred. On the other hand, Garrison wants to lend credibility to Douglass by promoting him as more than a former slave—as someone who excels in oratory and argumentation and who is fully capable of writing this book.

Letter from Wendall Phillips, Esq.

This letter written to Douglass by Wendall Phillips, a well-known Massachusetts abolitionist, also attempts to provide credibility to Douglass' narrative by referring to the length of time the two men have known each other and the feelings Phillips had when Douglass first told him his story.

Chapter One

In his opening chapter, Douglass recounts his birth into slavery in Tuckahoe, Maryland. His claim that he does not know his age other than a rough estimate of twenty-seven or twenty-eight is based on a common assumption by many slave owners that such information was unnecessary. Douglass goes on to explain his parentage. His mother is a dark-skinned slave named Harriet Bailey and his father is a white man. In fact, many believe that the master of the plantation is his father, a man whom Douglass calls Captain Anthony.

Douglass does not remember much of his mother, because they were separated at birth. He recalls several nights that she walked twelve miles from the plantation to which she had been sold to sleep by his side. Unfortunately, she dies when Douglass is seven. Douglass examines the implications of being the offspring of a slave owner.

> The master is frequently compelled
> to sell this class of his slaves, out of
> deference to the feelings of his white
> wife; and, cruel as the deed may
> strike any one to be ... it is often the
> dictate of humanity to do so."

The offspring of slaveholders are often punished cruelly by both masters and masters' sons, who are slaves' half-brothers. Douglass claims that slavery cannot last under such a system of interracial relations, where brothers are pitted against brothers, sons against fathers.

Douglass discusses the two masters he had in his lifetime and goes into some detail about Captain Anthony, his first master, who manages the Lloyd plantation. The overseer for Anthony, Mr. Plummer, is a particularly cruel man who beats Douglass' Aunt Hester for disobeying his command not to go out at night. Douglass ends the chapter by recounting his experience at a young age of witnessing his aunt being tied up and whipped by this overseer.

Chapter Two

In this chapter, Douglass continues to describe the conditions of being a slave on a plantation owned by Colonel Edward Lloyd, who owns a large estate in eastern Maryland. His master, Captain Anthony, runs the estate for Lloyd which, in Douglass' words, "had the appearance of a country village." Douglass gives details of what the slaves wear, where they sleep, and what they eat. He also describes several overseers that lord over them. One is Mr. Severe, who is unjust and cruel, and later arrives Mr. Hopkins, who dislikes dispensing physical punishment to the slaves.

In his famous passages about slave songs found in this chapter, Douglass describes the effects that their singing has on him, how despondent he felt and still feels when he thinks of those songs. They remind him not of inner joy as many northerners think but of deep and unbearable sadness. As he says, "Slaves sing most when they are most unhappy."

Chapter Three

Douglass describes different aspects of Colonel Lloyd's plantation. He begins with a description of Lloyd's garden, whose tasty fruits tempt slaves to eat from it. They are soundly punished for their transgressions. He discusses the unwarranted punishments that the slaves who take care of Colonel Lloyd's stables must undergo. He ends the chapter discussing the number of slaves Colonel Lloyd owns—close to one thousand—and how slaves must be careful about expressing any discontent they have with their owners. These comments may have severe repercussions. Douglass describes how slaves from different plantations often quarrel with each other on the merits of their owners.

Chapter Four

This chapter recounts a number of cruel and dehumanizing punishments that plantation slaves suffer at the hands of overseers such as Mr. Austin Gore. What is most disturbing about this chapter are Douglass' accounts of the numerous slave murders that occur. These are ignored by local judicial systems because the institution of slavery denies slaves basic human rights and legal protection. Douglass sums up this horrific disregard of the law by relaying a common saying among slaveholders "that it was worth a half-cent to kill a 'nigger,' and a half-cent to bury one."

Chapter Five

Here Douglass provides details of his treatment while living on the plantation of Colonel Lloyd. Because of his young age, he does not have to take on many of the responsibilities that come with adulthood. However, he suffers from hunger and lack of decent hygiene, clothes, and sleeping conditions. A sign of hope comes in the form of an opportunity to work for Hugh Auld, the brother of his old master's son-in-law. Douglass departs for Baltimore via ship and is introduced to his new mistress, Sophia Auld, and the Auld's young son, Thomas. Sophia is the first white person to treat him with warmth and friendliness. He views his move to Baltimore as a sign of providence that God is looking out for him, and that one day he will be free.

Chapter Six

Sophia Auld is described as being a kind and generous woman who never has owned a slave. She is a weaver by trade. Unlike most women of that era, especially in the South, Auld ran her own business until she married. She treats Douglass in a respectful and courteous manner, going so far as to teach him how to read. Unfortunately, her husband discovers this and forbids these lessons to continue. In thinking about Auld's harsh reaction, Douglass realizes that slaves' illiteracy allows the white man to retain power over slaves. As he states, "From that moment, I understood the pathway from slavery to freedom." Douglass sets himself the task of teaching himself to read and write. In this way, he hopes to become a free man. Douglass ends the chapter by comparing city and plantation slaves, noting that city slaves have the appearance of being free. They are better clothed and fed. Yet, ultimately, injustices and physical harm continue under slavery regardless of where the slave resides.

Chapter Seven

In this chapter, Douglass tells the reader that he lived with his master and mistress in Baltimore for seven years. Early on he realizes that Sophia, the mistress of the house, is falling under the spell of being a slave owner. In other words, her kind countenance is replaced with a stony one. She actively attempts to thwart his continued efforts to become literate. Douglass finds ways to learn to read from the white boys he talks to on the streets. He also finds books to read, such as *The Columbian Orator* that contain famous speeches. By reading these speeches that touch on questions of emancipation, Douglass engages himself in debating the arguments for and against emancipation. Yet as he becomes more learned, he also becomes more painfully aware of his dire circumstances—he is no better than a beast. This compels him to contemplate suicide. However, his growing literacy impels him to think of freedom as attainable. He makes an effort to teach himself to write in a variety of ways that avoid Sophia Auld's keen eye. Writing becomes an act of survival.

Chapter Eight

This short chapter covers significant changes in Douglass' life, as he tries to cope with his unstable position of a slave. Soon after moving to Baltimore, Douglass discovers that his former master's son, Richard, has died; three years later, Captain Anthony dies, leaving the estate to his only living children, Andrew and Lucretia. Douglass has to return to the plantation for a "valuation of the property" so that Anthony's property, including his slaves, can be divvied up.

Douglass discovers the horrors of being subjected to a thorough physical inspection and being parceled out to one of the two heirs of Captain Anthony's estate. Fortunately, Douglass is portioned to Lucretia and is allowed to return to Hugh Auld. Lucretia dies soon after his return to Baltimore, and soon thereafter Andrew also dies, leaving their slaves to the hands of strangers or abandoned. In particular, Douglass' grandmother is unable to be sold due to her old age and is left to die in the woods. This tragedy more than anything, Douglass states, "served to deepen my conviction of the infernal character of slavery, and to fill me with unutterable loathing of slaveholders." The chapter ends with Douglass being sent to work for Lucretia's husband, Thomas Auld, who has remarried and lives in rural Maryland. Once again, Douglass' future is uncertain and his hopes for escape appear bleak. Yet he plans on running away.

Chapter Nine

In March 1832, Douglass leaves Baltimore to live with Thomas Auld, whom Douglass knows from Colonel Lloyd's plantation. Auld and his new wife are cruel and unlikable people who keep their slaves always yearning for more food. Worse, Auld does not know how to treat his slaves in a consistent and respectful manner. "In all things noble which he attempted, his own meanness shone most conspicuous." Auld is also a pious man who participates in religious revivals and church goings-on, yet he is capable of great wrath and cruelty toward his slaves. Douglass mentions that Auld's preacher friends break up a school meeting set up for slaves by throwing sticks and missiles at them. Auld and Douglass do not see eye-to-eye. Eventually, after nine months of working for Auld, Douglass is sent to Mr. Covey, known as a 'negro-breaker,' to work for a year. Despite the horrors he has heard about working for Mr. Covey, Douglass looks forward to at least getting enough to eat.

Chapter Ten

In the longest chapter of the narrative, Douglass reveals some of the most distressing and empowering moments of his life as a slave. He begins the chapter illustrating how unfit he was to work as a field hand after having lived in the city for seven years. Douglass describes an incident where he has to drive a pair of unbroken oxen into the woods for some firewood. Because he takes too much time due to the surly nature of the oxen, Douglass gets whipped by Mr. Covey. Douglass goes on to describe the many ways in which Covey catches his slaves off guard by sneaking up on them. "He was under every tree, behind every stump, in every bush, and at every window, at the plantation." Because Covey is a poor man, he finds a way to double his slaveholdings by buying a female slave, who is then coupled with a hired hand to produce twins. Covey, Douglass claims, makes life miserable for every slave who comes in contact with him. Even on Sunday, his day off, Douglass can do nothing but bemoan his fate of being held hostage by Covey's emotional and physical torture.

However, Douglass and Covey have a confrontation that changes the power dynamic and provides Douglass with new energy for planning his escape. Douglass returns to Hugh Auld's home because of Covey's harsh treatment when Douglass fell ill. Douglass returns to Covey, due to his former master's lack of support and sympathy. Covey is so angry that Douglass runs back to the woods. This time he runs into a fellow slave, Sandy Jenkins. Jenkins gives Douglass a root that Jenkins claims will protect Douglass if he wears it on his right side. On Douglass' return, Covey acts kindly towards him. Several days later while Douglass is in the barn, Covey attempts to tie him up for a whipping. It is then that Douglass begins to fight back. A tremendous battle ensues that lasts for two hours, and eventually Covey retreats. For the next six months, Covey does not lay a finger on Douglass.

Douglass then discusses how slaves are free from Christmas to New Year's Day. They are encouraged to drink excessively by slaveholders so that on returning to work, the slaves are relieved that they do not have to indulge again. Encouraging slaves to drink is done, Douglass explains, so that freedom is perceived in its worst possible mode.

After Douglass finishes at Covey's, he goes to work for Mr. William Freeland, who turns out to be kinder than most slaveholders. While there, Douglass begins to teach Freeland's two slaves, Henry and John Harris, and many other slaves in the area how to read and write. Among these slaves Douglass makes some very close ties, and with several of them, he begins to plot out a way to escape to the North. However, their plans go awry when someone betrays them and they end up in jail.

A week later, Douglass is sent back to Baltimore, where he again takes up residence with Hugh Auld. While there, Douglass begins to work for Mr. Gardner, who runs a shipbuilding yard. After eight months he is subjected to racial slander and prejudice by four carpenters, who attempt to beat him to death. From that time on, he begins to work as a caulker in the shipyards. He makes a great deal of money but has to hand it over to Hugh Auld. Douglass sets his hopes on escaping to the North, where he can work and keep the wages that he earns.

Chapter Eleven

In his last chapter, Douglass achieves his goal of attaining freedom in the North. Working as a caulker provides Douglass with a number of advantages he never had working on a plantation, but he is still very troubled by his lack of freedom. Although Douglass has achieved an ideal situation for a slave, he wants what his masters have: the ability to do what, and go where, they please, answering to nobody. With this in mind, Douglass continues working in the shipyards. He bargains with Hugh Auld to keep his wages and promises to pay Auld for his own time as well as his food and lodging each week. The bargain creates conflict between Douglass and Auld; Auld thwarts Douglass' attempt to be independent of him. Douglass escapes to the North and reaches New York on September 3, 1838. The reader is not given many details of Douglass' escape, as he does not want to endanger the lives of other slaves seeking freedom in a similar way. In fact, Douglass makes it clear that others have spoken too openly about the underground railroad, the famous escape route that many slaves use to reach the North, and have jeopardized slaves' and abolitionists' lives because of this.

Arriving in New York, Douglass is overwhelmed by his new status and surroundings. His initial enthusiasm is tempered by fear that he may be sent back to Baltimore if caught. After a few lonely days, Douglass is introduced to David Ruggles, an African-American journalist and abolitionist, who helps Douglass plan to settle in New Bedford, Massachusetts. Douglass and his fiancée, Anna Murray, marry. Afterwards, they set off for New Bedford, where they stay with Mr. and Mrs. Nathan Johnson. The Johnsons suggest that Douglass change his name, currently Frederick Augustus Washington Bailey. He decides on Douglass after the character Lord James of Douglas in Sir Walter Scott's poem "Lady of the Lake." After living in New Bedford, Douglass notes that his expectations of the North contrast with what he sees around him. Not only do people seem happier and healthier, but those who are not wealthy seem to be well fed and well housed. Even African Americans who had been slaves appear to live better than many slaveholders Douglass has known. Douglass soon finds work, though he runs across prejudice when he tries to work as a caulker.

Douglass ends this chapter with his discovery of the abolitionist newspaper (published by William Lloyd Garrison) called the *Liberator*, which he devours. "The paper became my meat and drink." By reading this paper, Douglass educates himself and soon becomes involved in the antislavery movement. The narrative ends with Douglass giving a speech at an antislavery convention in Nantucket, Massachusetts, where he first begins to recount his misfortunes and fortunes as a slave.

Appendix

In this important appendix to his work, Douglass attempts to explain his harsh condemnation of Christianity as practiced by southern slaveholders. As he explains it, "Revivals of religion and revivals in the slave-trade go hand in hand together." Douglass points out the un-Christian lack of awareness that slaveholders have in understanding their participation in a system that condemns a group of people to a despairing and inhumane existence. He makes his point clear when he explains how many of the pious slaveholders are more than willing to donate money and pray for those who live in other parts of the world. However, they do little to bestow any spiritual or material generosity on those whom they own. He ends the appendix with a parody of a church hymn. It depicts in gruesome fashion the incongruity of southern Christians who appear to be pious but have little moral courage or stamina to end an elitist system that benefits only slaveholders.

Master Andrew

Andrew is Captain Anthony's son, who is a wicked and merciless drunk that many slaves on Lloyd's plantation fear because he is so ruthless and cruel.

Captain Anthony

Captain Anthony is Douglass' first master and owns him until Anthony dies. Captain Anthony does not play a large part in the actual narrative, yet Douglass' life is thrown into disarray after Anthony dies, since he is bounced from one relative of Anthony to the next. Moreover, Douglass suggests early on that the captain may be his father. Douglass undergoes many hardships due to his owner's not providing for him, and thus he is at the mercy of Anthony's two children, Lucretia and Andrew, and their offspring.

Mr. Hugh Auld

Hugh Auld is the brother of Captain Anthony's son-in-law, Captain Thomas Auld. Beginning as a teenager, Douglass works for Auld for seven years in Baltimore, mostly taking care of Auld's son, Thomas. As slave masters go, Auld is less violent and more fair toward Douglass than many others he has worked under, yet Auld forbids his wife, Sophia, to teach Douglass how to read. He claims that education "would forever unfit him to be a slave." Auld eventually and unwittingly provides Douglass the means of escape by hiring him out to ship carpenters.

Mrs. Sophia Auld

Mrs. Sophia Auld is a weaver by trade and married to Hugh Auld. She plays a significant part in Douglass' literacy acquisition by teaching him the alphabet. Unfortunately, she stops when her husband finds out and explains, "If you give a nigger an inch, he will take an ell." Afterwards, Sophia becomes cold and mean-spirited towards Douglass, treating him callously like other slave owners. Yet ultimately she proves to be the nicest of Douglass' many masters.

Master Thomas Auld

Thomas Auld is the brother of Hugh Auld, whom Douglass worked for in Baltimore, and the former husband of Lucretia, daughter of Douglass' master Captain Anthony. Because of a severe misunderstanding between the two brothers, Thomas Auld in spite takes Douglass to live with him for two years in St. Michael's, a rural part of Maryland. These are the worst years of Douglass' life, as he endures extreme hardship, both physically and mentally. Auld is most known for keeping his slaves hungry.

Harriet Bailey

Harriet Bailey is Frederick Douglass' mother. Despite being separated from her son at his birth, Harriet attempts to see her infant son by walking twelve miles from the farm where she works as a field hand to stay with him for a few hours before walking back before sunrise. She dies when Douglass is about seven years old.

Edward Covey

Edward Covey was known as "a well-known negro breaker and slave-driver" in the St. Michael's area of Maryland, where Thomas Auld lived. His reputation in the area provides him with a steady supply of slaves who need to be taught who is master. Thus, Covey employs harsh and unrelenting physical work and punishment to break a slave's spirit and transform him into a brute. Ironically and hypocritically, Covey professes to be "a pious soul." Covey is known by the slaves who work for him as "a snake" because he sneaks up on slaves when they least expect it. Douglass is sent to Covey for a year as a field hand, where he undergoes the worst trials his spirit has ever undergone. Yet having reached his lowest point, Douglass stands up to the man who has reduced him to merely an animal by challenging him on his own ground. After a grueling fight in which Douglass has the upper hand, Covey never again whips Douglass.

Frederick Douglass

Douglass is the narrator of his account as a slave and his eventual journey to freedom. Beginning from his birth, Douglass experiences and witnesses many hardships throughout his years as a slave in Maryland and is prone to misfortune due to his subjugated status. His attempts at liberating himself, first through self-education and then through his escape to the North, are a testament to the desire of humans to acquire freedom.

William Freeland

William Freeland is another slaveholder whom Douglass works for in the St. Michael's area of Maryland. However, he is far more open and prudent than any other slaveholder Douglass has known. He never professes to be heavily religious or pious, nor does he work slaves to complete exhaustion. Freeland also owns only two slaves, Henry Harris and John Harris. In the year that Douglass works for him, he never receives one blow.

Mr. William Gardner

Gardner is a shipbuilder who hires Douglass to work for him and whose shipyard is fraught with racial tension between black and white workers.

William Lloyd Garrison

At the beginning of the narrative, William Garrison writes a preface that is meant to lend credibility to Frederick Douglass' slave narrative. Because of the prejudice that many northerners had toward African Americans, Garrison felt it important to lend his own credibility as a show of support to Douglass.

The Grandmother

Although the reader never knows her real name, the grandmother of Frederick Douglass is an emblematic figure of the dehumanizing effects of slavery on women. She is born into slavery, has borne twelve children into slavery, and dies a slave, yet her numerous contributions to the plantation are rewarded with any number of cruelties. After taking care of Captain Anthony from the time he was a baby to when he died, as well as caring for her many children and grandchildren, the grandmother is left to fend for herself in the wilds of nature. Too old to work, she has been let out to die.

Media Adaptations

- *Frederick Douglass,* part of Biography Series, available from A & E Television Network, is a fifty-minute video exploring the life of Douglass, with critical comments from biographers, historians, and African-American scholars.

- *Frederick Douglass: 1818-1895: Abolitionist Editor,* part of *The Black Americans of Achievement Video Collection* (1992), is a concise, comprehensive portrait of Douglass' major life accomplishments as a writer, editor, and abolitionist activist. Directed by Rhonda Fabian and Jerry Baber, the piece runs thirty minutes and is available from Schlessinger Video

Productions.

- *Frederick Douglass: When the Lion Wrote History,* a PBS video production, provides an extensive historical and cultural background to Douglass' life from his life as a slave to his lifelong project to provide equal rights and protection to African Americans. It is directed by Orlando Bagwell, 1994.

- *Narrative of the Life of Frederick Douglass* is an audiotape published by Recorded Books. Charles Turner reads the entire narrative, with a running time of four hours and thirty-one minutes.

Henry Harris

Henry Harris is a slave of Mr. Freeland who, along with Douglass and others, plans to escape to the North. Douglass teaches him to read and write.

John Harris

See Henry Harris

Aunt Hester

Aunt Hester is a relative of Douglass who is whipped mercilessly by Mr. Plummer, an overseer.

At a young age, Douglass witnesses his aunt being tied up and whipped until the blood drips to the floor for going out to meet a young black man on another farm. This is the first time Douglass realizes the horrors of slavery.

Sandy Jenkins

Sandy Jenkins, a slave whom Douglass meets in the woods after running away from Covey's farm, gives Douglass a root to carry on his right side that she says will protect him from physical harm.

Colonel Edward Lloyd

Colonel Lloyd owns the plantation on which Douglass is born in eastern Maryland. He is mostly mentioned in the *Narrative* in terms of what he owns and how he treats his slaves who take care of his horses. His plantation is described by Douglass as being as large as a village, and his slaveholdings are close to five hundred.

Anna Murray

Though she is mentioned only briefly in the narrative, Anna Murray is a domestic worker in Baltimore who moves to New York to marry Douglass soon after they arrive there. She is a free worker and helps fund Douglass' journey to freedom.

David Ruggles

An African-American abolitionist and journalist, David Ruggles befriends Douglass soon after Douglass' arrival in New York and helps him and Anna settle in New Bedford, Massachusetts.

An Argument Against Slavery

One of the most explicit themes of the *Narrative* is the oppressive effect of institutionalized racism in the form of slavery in the southern United States. Throughout the narrative, Douglass provides striking examples of how slaves are brutalized, mentally and physically, by the slaveholding system. His narrative provides numerous examples that add up to a powerful indictment of the dehumanizing effects of slavery. These include the physical abuse of women, as in the treatment of Douglass' Aunt Hester, and the separation of families. Douglass points out that slavery is not only harmful to slaves but affects slaveholders too. His greatest example of the damaging effects of slavery on slaveholders is that of Sophia Auld. Auld had never been a slaveholder and is at first kind to Douglass. By owning him, she retracts her generosity of spirit. As Douglass notes, "The fatal poison of irresponsible power was already in her hands, and soon commenced its infernal work."

False versus True Christianity

Another theme that runs throughout the *Narrative* is what it means to be a Christian in the South when slavery is at its core immoral. Douglass ingeniously sets up a dichotomy between two kinds of Christianity, as noted by scholars Keith Miller and Ruth Ellen Kocher in "Shattering Kidnapper's Heavenly Union: Interargumentation in Douglass's Oratory": "He constantly pits True Christianity, which he explicitly embraces, against the False Christianity of racism and slavery." This theme is found in the depictions of cruel masters. These masters beat their slaves to near death but appear pious by attending church regularly, giving to charities, and becoming ministers. The appendix reveals how Christianity, as practiced in the South, has slavery as its ugly accomplice. By juxtaposing images of slavery with religious piety, Douglass reveals how the two cannot be separated. "The slave auctioneer's bell and the church-going bell chime in with each other, and the bitter cries of the heart-broken slave are drowned in the religious shouts of his pious master."

Importance of Literacy to the Concept of Freedom

As a young boy, Douglass is taught the alphabet by his mistress, Sophia Auld. After she is prohibited to continue by her husband, Douglass finds ways to continue his education by interacting with Anglos. Literacy leads Douglass to see freedom as a goal that can be attained. For example, his purchase of *The Columbian Orator,* a book of political speeches written by ancient orators and Enlightenment thinkers, introduces him to the art of oration. He uses this skill later in life as an abolitionist activist. Reading such books makes him wonder why he was excluded from those rights granted to his white master. "The reading of these documents enabled me to utter my thoughts, and to meet the arguments brought forward to sustain slavery...." Douglass' education contributes to his understanding of the injustices done to him and all slaves. It fosters a desire in him for freedom. His education leads to a restlessness that will not be quieted by physical beatings or hard labor. Eventually, his education leads him to escape slavery.

Achieving Selfhood

In many ways, the *Narrative* is a coming-of-age story that depicts Douglass achieving his freedom and acquiring a sense of self. One of the most powerful lines in the *Narrative* comes in chapter ten before the showdown between Douglass and Mr. Covey. Douglass directly addresses the relationship between slavery and the denial of manhood when he says, "You have seen how a man was made a slave; you shall see how a slave was made a man." Because slavery was bound up in denying full selfhood to both men and women, many slaves were denied the ability to perceive themselves as full human beings. Douglass' narrative shows how attaining control of one's life through freedom is necessary to achieving selfhood, or, in Douglass' case, manhood.

Topics for Further Study

- In the 1840s, when Douglass wrote his antislavery narrative, the abolitionist movement was gaining momentum in both the United States and Great Britain. However, unlike today, communication methods were limited. Research the abolitionist movement of this time and discuss the communication methods that abolitionists used to spread the antislavery message.

- At the same time that abolitionists were calling for the end of slavery, women in the United States were beginning to organize around equal rights. This First Wave of feminism was closely linked to the abolitionist movement. Research the relationship that the abolitionist movement had with First Wave feminism. How were their goals similar? Where did they part? How was Douglass involved in the First Wave feminist movement?

- Since Douglass wrote his *Narrative*, many other African Americans have written autobiographies that use their own experiences to critique American society's marginalization of them. What other groups in the United States have used the genre of autobiography in this manner? When were these books written and what was their mission?

- Published in the 1960s, *The Autobiography of Malcolm X* had the same crossover appeal that Douglass' *Narrative* did in terms of attracting both African-American and white audiences. Read excerpts from the book and draw comparisons between the two books. For example, what themes do the two books address? How do they differ? How are they the same?

- Harriet Jacobs' *Incidents in the Life of a Slave Girl,* published in 1861, is the mostly highly acclaimed slave narrative written by a woman. Read it, and then compare and contrast it with the *Narrative*. In particular, analyze how gender accounts for specific experiences undergone as a slave. Then discuss differences in narrative structure, themes, and literary devices in the texts.

- Explore more thoroughly the differences that Douglass brings to light between being a plantation slave and a city slave by researching historical documents and books that describe what life was like in these two different environments.

Style

The lasting political, emotional, and dramatic power of the *Narrative of the Life of Frederick Douglass* stems not only from the highly controversial subject matter of slavery but also from Douglass' ability to utilize a number of literary and rhetorical devices that enable him to create a compelling and complex testimony to the horrific nature of slavery. One of Douglass' notable literary devices is his ability to render an engaging narrative plot in highly descriptive language. The descriptions include particular incidents, people, and moments in his life as a slave. His descriptions lend a particular credibility to his story by fostering graphic images and scenes that are difficult to forget. Once read, who can forget the image that Douglass invokes of the whipping of his Aunt Hester at the end of first chapter? In fact, as scholar Jeffrey Steele argues in his article "Douglass and Sentimental Rhetoric," Douglass assumed that through these images his readers would "identify with and feel the pain of those in bondage." Readers are persuaded by his narrative that slavery is immoral and wrong.

The scholar Gregory Lampe, in *Frederick Douglass: Freedom's Voice, 1818-1845,* claims that Douglass was primarily an orator, one who argued against slavery through his use of narrative. "As in his antislavery speeches, his autobiography went beyond simply narrating his slave experiences and exhorted his audience to act against the slaveholder's vile corruption." If one views the *Narrative* as an argument, then the strength of Douglass' style is his use of rhetoric to convince his readers to join efforts to abolish slavery. Douglass' sophisticated argumentation involves using emotional appeals, found in many of his descriptions. For example, in chapter eight, Douglass describes the slow and lonely death of his grandmother, who has been abandoned by her master and left to die in the woods. "She stands— she sits—she falls—she groans—she dies." Although these sentences are simple in their construction, they create a powerful scene when strung together, attached by dashes that imply pauses between the grandmother's movements.

Besides his ability to argue emotionally, Douglass also uses logical and ethical appeals throughout the *Narrative*, dismantling many arguments and misconceptions that slaveholders relied upon to justify the slave system in the South. He does this using himself as an example that defies many of these arguments. For example, a primary argument used to justify slavery was that African Americans were biologically inferior and mentally deficient to whites. Yet Douglass defies this misconception by revealing that this myth was perpetuated by denying slaves the right to read and write. Douglass has this insight when he is denied the right to read by his master, Hugh Auld. By providing himself as an example that overturns many of these arguments, Douglass makes a convincing case for the abolishment of slavery.

Besides rhetorical abilities, Douglass also relies on a number of literary devices that add to the power of his narrative. Devices described by Lampe in *Frederick Douglass: Freedom's Voice, 1818-1845* include biblical allusion, metaphor, parody (as found in the church hymn that he adapts to suit southern slaveholders in the appendix), and rhetorical devices such as alliteration, repetition, antithesis, and simile.

Imagery

One of the most convincing devices that Douglass utilizes in the *Narrative* is animal imagery. Such imagery reveals the dehumanizing effects of slavery in both slaveholders and slaves, especially in the rural context of the plantation system, where slaves were chattel, similar to domesticated animals. These images include similes (such as describing the young children feeding at a trough as being "like so many pigs") and association (as in chapter eight, when Douglass describes the slaves' experience at the valuation as being "on the same rank in scale" of "horses, sheep and swine"). Douglass makes it clear that slaves were not only viewed as being animals, but they also lived in conditions that reinforced that stereotype. However, Douglass, in a clever move, uses animal metaphor to suggest that slave owners were not exempt from being perceived as animals by slaves themselves. For example, Mr. Covey is known by slaves who work for him as "the snake." After Douglass' escape, Douglass feels like "one who had escaped a den of hungry lions." The animal imagery Douglass uses is complicated by the system of slavery that produced bestial behavior regardless of race.

Tone

To many contemporary readers, Douglass' writing style in the *Narrative* may appear overly emotional and overwritten in its description of suffering and hardship. For example, in chapter ten, Douglass plaintively describes the ships sailing on the Chesapeake Bay as "beautiful vessels, robed in that purest white, so delightful to the eye of freemen" "were to me so many shrouded ghosts." Yet Douglass was very aware of the popularity of a writing style in the mid-nineteenth century called "sentimental rhetoric," primarily used by middle-class women writers as a way of engaging readers directly with their subject matter. Douglass may have been able to engage readers not sympathetic with slavery's victims by appealing to their hearts for freedom and justice. In other words, as Steele in his article "Douglass and Sentimental Rhetoric" notes, in order to get white audiences to trust him as a narrator, Douglass used sentimental language as a means of representing himself "as a man of reason, moral principle, religious faith, and sentiment."

Slave Narratives

Douglass' *Narrative* was part of a growing literary genre. This type of writing, which used common conventions, came to be known as "slave narratives." The American-based genre grew out of the harsh conditions imposed by the slave society of the New World—the denial of freedom to African Americans. Once free, many slaves, rather than turn their backs on their past, fought hard to abolish enslavement by writing of their experiences. In his introduction to *The Classic Slave Narratives,* scholar Henry Louis Gates provides a compelling history of the formation of this particular African-American literary tradition. Gates claims that "the black slave's narrative came to be a communal utterance, a collective tale rather than merely an individual's autobiography." Slave narratives were written primarily as a testament to the horrors of slavery and the slave's ability to transcend such hardships. Works of this genre, as noted in "Framing the Slave Narrative / Framing Discussion," by scholar Russ Castronovo, "seek to educate a largely white audience about the horrors of slavery by revealing what the fugitive has learned during his or her 'career' as a slave."

Historical Context

In the mid-nineteenth century, when Douglass wrote the *Narrative*, the United States was becoming divided over the issue of slavery. In the North, a growing abolitionist movement that had started in the late eighteenth century began to gather momentum as its leaders made every effort to spread their antislavery message. They held meetings, gave lectures, published antislavery newspapers, and traveled across the country to spread their message. Meanwhile, in the South, slaveholders rigidly held on to their view that slaves were useful only as laborers that helped sustain their agricultural economy. White people, in both the North and the South, continued to treat slaves as inferior beings, in most cases denying them any legal protection.

However, as more slaves found their way to freedom in the North, either through the assistance of the Underground Railroad or their own inventive methods, they began to write of their experiences under slavery. These 'slave narratives' became popular as adventure stories and a kind of protest literature. Although slaves had written of their experiences since slavery's inception in the United States (in the late eighteenth century), their stories were not widely read until the 1830s when heated political debates over slavery became widespread. Moreover, the abolishment of slavery in the British Empire in 1833 fanned the desire of many

Americans for slavery to end.

Douglass' *Narrative*, published in 1845, contributed to the growing protest literature in the North that pleaded for the end of slavery. As a major African-American speaker in the abolitionist movement, Douglass became a central figurehead for the cause. Articulate, educated, morally upstanding, and self-possessing, Douglass dispelled many myths that both Northerners and Southerner held about African Americans. In his book *On Racial Frontiers: The New Culture of Frederick Douglass, Ralph Ellison, and Bob Marley,* scholar Gregory Stephens notes that "Frederick Douglass articulated most clearly, on an international level, what was at stake in the abolitionist movement(s)." Similar to African-American political leaders that came after him, such as Booker T. Washington, W. E. B. DuBois, Malcolm X, and Martin Luther King, Douglass carved out a public space for African-American voices to be heard and for their rights to fought over and won.

In 1845, when Douglass published his narrative, African-American slaves did not have much representation legally or socially. They could not participate in public office nor could they vote. Their legal protection in the North was limited; in the South, nonexistent. Slave narratives such as Douglass' contributed to a growing literature base produced by African Americans that resisted negative portrayals and stereotypes through self-representation. Publishing antislavery documents in the North was one of the few ways that African-

American voices could be heard. As Russ Castronovo claims, in his article, "Framing the Slave Narrative / Framing the Discussion," "The slave narrative refutes the dominant cultural authority that insisted slaves could not write about … or rightfully criticize United States domestic institutions." In fact, argumentative narratives such as Douglass' were one of the few methods of non-violent resistance available. Although slave uprisings occurred in the southern United States, usually they were quashed. During Douglass' time, an attempt to attack the slaveholding South took place in 1856 at Harper's Ferry, Virginia, when John Brown—a white abolitionist leader and friend of Douglass—along with twenty-one followers captured the U.S. arsenal. They were gunned down by the U.S. Marines. Brown, who survived, was hanged for treason not long after this attack.

Tensions mounted between pro-slavery and antislavery forces when a devastating law was passed in 1850 called the Fugitive Slave Law. It penalized those who assisted runaway slaves and allowed escaped slaves to be tracked down and returned to their ex-slaveholders. Some time later, in 1857, the Dred Scott ruling handed down by the Supreme Court decided that African Americans had no legal protection under the Constitution. This climate only increased abolitionists' motivations to protest more vehemently and support politicians willing to promote the freeing of slaves. Though many years away when the *Narrative* was published, the election of President Lincoln in 1860, the declaration of Civil War in 1861, and the

Emancipation Proclamation delivered in 1863 were all decisive events that formed a backdrop to the fight for political and legal representation undertaken by African Americans like Douglass.

Compare & Contrast

- **1840s:** Douglass and other abolitionists campaign around the country to abolish slavery, speaking of its horrors and promoting the rights of African Americans to be granted legal and political representation.

  Today: African Americans and other minority populations have legal protection and equal opportunities in all aspects of life, even though racial discrimination continues to occur.

- **1840s:** Douglass is one of the first African-American public intellectuals to bring issues of race and inequality to the forefront of political life in the United States and works closely with presidents to achieve equal rights for African Americans.

  Today: African Americans are represented in high political offices by newly elected Secretary of State

Colin Powell and National Security Advisor Condoleeza Rice as well as in academic life by intellectuals such as Cornel West, Patricia Williams, and Henry Louis Gates.

- **1840s:** A growing and increasingly literate American population devours popular literature such as slave narratives, adventure novels, and captive narratives.

  Today: Popular literature continues to be read in the form of suspense, mystery, romance, and horror novels.

- **1840s:** Douglass travels from state to state protesting the evils of slavery and continues to speak for African-American rights until he dies. Many of his speeches are recorded and distributed in newspapers.

  Today: Hip hop artists such as Ice T and Lauren Hill expose the continuing injustices of racial discrimination in their songwriting. They send their message via live performance and recordings.

Although its importance as an historical document that details the horrors of slavery cannot be denied, the *Narrative* has also become part of the American literary canon. It is taught widely in literature classes as an exemplary nineteenth-century American literary text and takes its place among others published at the same time, such as Thoreau's *Walden,* Stowe's *Uncle Tom's Cabin,* Melville's *Moby Dick,* and Alcott's *Little Women.* However, its contribution to the growth of an African-American literary tradition and to the emergence of an African-American identity form a large part of its cultural significance today.

Critical Overview

Amazingly enough, slave narratives fell into obscurity towards the end of the nineteenth century, despite their testimonies to the cruel and unjust treatment of slaves by southern slaveholders and their enormous popularity. It was not until the mid-twentieth century that scholars began to investigate slave narratives as literature in their own right. The combination of personal testimony, cultural history, autobiography, antislavery rhetoric, and adventure story created a genre that marked the beginning of an African-American literary tradition. In their preface to the Norton Critical Edition of *Narrative of the Life of Frederick Douglass*, editors William Andrews and William McFeely write that "The heightened civil rights militancy of the 1960s, along with the rise of Black Studies in the academy, helped resurrect the *Narrative* and elevate Douglass to prominence as the key figure in the evolution of African-American prose in the antebellum period." With the growth of a body of work defined as the African-American literary canon, Douglass' writings were again at the center of attention.

Douglass' adoption into the canon was the product of a growing body of African-American Studies scholars interested in investigating the origins of African-American political, cultural, and literary thought. For example, American Studies professor Albert E. Stone claims in "Identity and Art in Frederick Douglass' *Narrative*" that the

Narrative is the precursor to African-American autobiographies such as Richard Wright's *Black Boy*, Malcolm X's (and Haley's) *The Autobiography of Malcolm X*, and Angelou's *I Know Why the Caged Bird Sings*.

At the time of the *Narrative*'s publication in 1845, the United States was becoming increasingly divided over the issue of slavery. Years prior to his writing of the *Narrative*, Douglass campaigned against slavery, often telling the narrative he eventually penned as part of his oratory. The *Narrative* made Douglass a celebrity nationally and internationally, selling 4,500 copies in its first five months of publication. Margaret Fuller, editor of the *Dial*, had this to say about its publication: "We wish that every one may read his book and see what a mind might have been stifled in bondage."

However, not everyone was pleased or convinced by Douglass' depiction of his life as a former slave. His most vehement critics attempted to undermine his credibility as an author because of his racial identity as well as his former status as a slave. That an African-American ex-slave who had no formal education could write a book that was eloquent and stirring as well as logical and insightful was hard to fathom by many white Americans, both in the South and the North. The most famous attack came from A. C. C. Thompson, a slaveholder who lived near the home of Thomas Auld, where Douglass had been a slave for many years. In his accusatory letter published in the abolitionist paper *The Liberator*, Thompson disputes many of Douglass' claims about slavery as well as his personal accounts of Maryland slaveholders whom he labored under. Douglass, however, saw this attack as an opportunity to grant even more legitimacy to his narrative and wrote a reply several months later that uncovered the duplicity and lies of Thompson's letter. Thus, the *Narrative* had an exciting and controversial reception that has been diminished over time but reveals the power of the word to incite action and change.

Sources

Andrews, William L., and William S. McFeely, eds., Preface, in *Narrative of the Life of Frederick Douglass, An American Slave, Written by Himself*, W. W. Norton & Company, 1997, p. ix.

Castronovo, Russ, "Framing the Slave Narrative / Framing the Discussion," in *Approaches to Teaching Narrative of the Life of Frederick Douglass,* edited by James C. Hall, Modern Language Association, 1999, pp. 43, 47.

Fuller, Margaret, Review, in *Narrative of the Life of Frederick Douglass, An American Slave, Written by Himself*, edited by William L. Andrews and William S. McFeely, W. W. Norton & Company, 1997, pp. 83-85.

Gates, Henry Louis, Jr., ed., Introduction to *The Classic Slave Narratives,* Mentor Books, 1987, pp. x, xiii.

Lampe, Gregory P., *Frederick Douglass: Freedom's Voice, 1818-1845,* Michigan State University Press, 1998, pp. 269, 289.

McDowell, Deborah E., "In the First Place: Making Frederick Douglass and the Afro-American Narrative Tradition," in *Narrative of the Life of Frederick Douglass, An American Slave, Written by Himself*, edited by William L. Andrews and William S. McFeely, W. W. Norton & Company, 1997, pp. 178-179.

Miller, Keith, and Ruth Ellen Kocher, "Shattering Kidnapper's Heavenly Union: Interargumentation in Douglass's Oratory," in *Approaches to Teaching Narrative of the Life of Frederick Douglass,* edited by James C. Hall, Modern Language Association, 1999, p. 83.

Moses, Wilson J., "Writing Freely? Frederick Douglass and the Constraints of Racialized Writing," in *Frederick Douglass: New Literary and Historical Essays,* edited by Eric J. Sundquist, Cambridge University Press, 1990, p. 69.

Niemtzow, Annette, "The Problematic of Self in Autobiography: The Example of the Slave Narrative," in *Frederick Douglass's Narrative of the Life of Frederick Douglass,* edited by Harold Bloom, Chelsea House, 1988, p. 116.

Steele, Jeffrey, "Douglass and Sentimental Rhetoric," in *Approaches to Teaching Narrative of the Life of Frederick Douglass,* edited by James C. Hall, Modern Language Association, 1999, pp. 68, 72.

Stephens, Gregory, *On Racial Frontiers: The New Culture of Frederick Douglass, Ralph Ellison, and Bob Marley,* Cambridge University Press, 1999, p. 57.

Stone, Albert E., "Art and Identity in Frederick Douglass's *Narrative,*" in *Frederick Douglass's Narrative of the Life of Frederick Douglass,* edited by Harold Bloom, Chelsea House, 1988, pp. 11-12, 27.

Taylor, Yuval, Introduction to *I Was Born a Slave: An Anthology of Classic Slave Narratives, Volume One, 1772-1849,* edited by Yuval Taylor, Lawrence Hill Books, 1999, p. xviii.

Thompson, A. C. C., "Letter from a Former Slaveholder," in *Narrative of the Life of Frederick Douglass, An American Slave, Written by Himself,* edited by William L. Andrews and William S. McFeely, W. W. Norton & Company, 1997, pp. 88-91.

Further Reading

Blassingame, John W., *The Slave Community: Plantation Life in the Antebellum South,* Oxford University Press, 1979.

> This historical and cultural study focuses particularly on the lives of plantation slaves in the South, detailing their daily lives and the constraints, impositions, and harsh realities they had to overcome in order to create a community.

Davis, Charles T., and Henry Louis Gates, Jr., *The Slave's Narrative,* Oxford University Press, 1985.

> This selection of essays, responses, and critical reviews analyzes and discusses the genre of slave narratives.

Foster, Frances Smith, *Witnessing Slavery: The Development of Ante-Bellum Slave Narratives,* 2d ed., University of Wisconsin Press, 1994.

> This classic study of slave narratives analyzes the social, political, and literary aspects of this particularly African-American genre.

Genovese, Eugene D., *Roll, Jordan, Roll: The World the Slaves Made,* Vintage Books, 1976.

> This thorough account of the

institution of slavery in the United States covers economics, psychology, politics, sociology, and geography.

McFeeley, William, *Frederick Douglass,* Norton, 1991.

This comprehensive and highly respected biography details the many aspects of Douglass' life.

Miller, Douglas T., *Frederick Douglass and the Fight for Freedom,* Facts on File Publications, 1988.

Miller provides a generalized biographical account of Douglass' rich and varied life.

9 781375 399791